From the Books of
Jane Dodson

The ABCs of Needlepoint

Books by Hope Hanley

HOPE HANLEY

The ABCs
of
Needlepoint

Drawings by Trudy Nicholson
Photographs by Allen Bress
except where otherwise indicated

Charles Scribner's Sons / New York

Printed in the United States of America
Library of Congress Catalog Card Number 73-1099
SBN 684-13511-6 (cloth)

This fierce leopard cub was worked on penelope canvas by Louis
J. Gartner, Jr. of Palm Beach, Florida. Mr. Gartner separated the
canvas threads to give a double count for the cub itself, the background was worked over the two threads. The judicious use of shading gives the cub its three dimensional look.

Acknowledgments

WRITING is one occupation where friends are important to accomplishing your job. Friends offer encouragement, suggestions and well-meant criticism. I would like to express my gratitude to the following friends, in Washington, Dorothy Burchette, Aileen Sterling, Françoise Woodard, and Inez Fowler; in Middleburg, Virginia, Rosalie Grasty, Betty Boteler and Evelyn McConnell; and in Atlanta, Georgia, Augusta Horsey. Having a wonderfully sympathetic editor like Elinor Parker is a great help too.

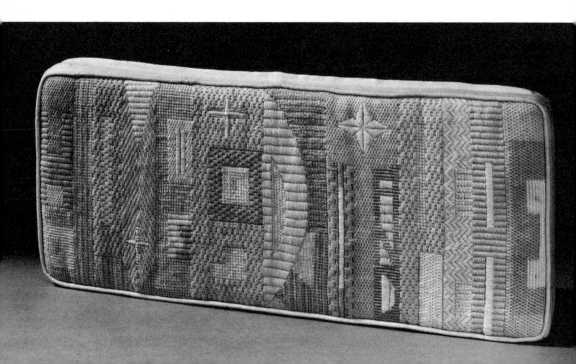

Preface

THIS BOOK was written to teach needlepoint to beginners, whether they have a teacher or are self taught. It is by no means an encyclopedia, but it is hoped that the book will adequately answer the questions that bother beginning needlepointers. The first chapter covers materials, the mechanics of starting a canvas, and the basic stitch. This is an important chapter for beginners and a review for old hands. The second chapter explains design and color as it pertains to needlepoint and the techniques and media used to apply design and color to canvas. The third chapter covers twenty fancy stitches, telling which canvases they like and some of their idiosyncrasies. The last chapter deals with methods of blocking needlepoint, different ways of finishing projects, trims, and how to make repairs to damaged canvases.

Ruth Klausmeyer of the Needlework Studio of Cincinnati, Ohio, designed and worked this kneeler for her son's wedding. It was worked in various stitches in shades of white. It reads "The Love of God Joy and Peace."

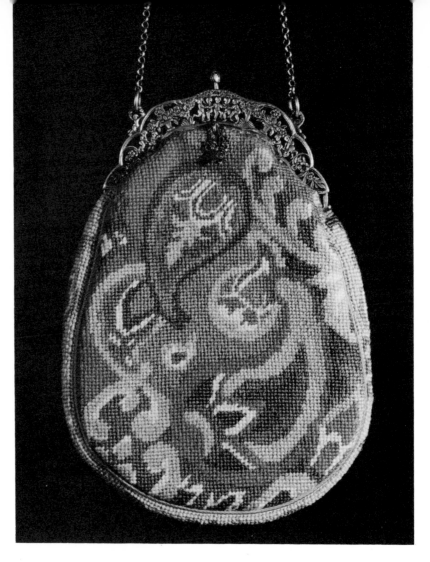

Mrs. Thomas Carroll of Chevy Chase worked this bag for an antique silver frame. It was designed by Aileen Sterling.

Chapter One

NEEDLEPOINT has been considered an enjoyable pastime since the days of Queen Elizabeth, when it was called tent stitch. In the early nineteenth century, the increased leisure time of ladies set off a fad for needlepoint, then known as Berlin work. Today, it is popularly called needlepoint in the United States, and in England the craft is known as canvas work. Needlepoint is embroidery worked with a needle over the threads of an open-weave material called canvas.

Canvas

Canvas is usually made of highly sized cotton in white, ecru, yellow, and a pinkish yellow. At present most of it is woven in Europe. Most canvas purchased by the yard is about forty inches wide; however, it may be had from twenty-eight inches to fifty-four inches wide. Canvas is woven as evenly as possible with a certain number of threads per inch. These threads are often called mesh. Canvas is available from $3\frac{1}{2}$ mesh per inch to 30 mesh per inch. The most commonly used are 10, 12, 14, and 18 mesh per inch. Any canvas over 16 mesh is considered to be petit point.

There are three different weaves of canvas: mono-canvas, two-thread and penelope, and leno canvas. Mono canvas is a

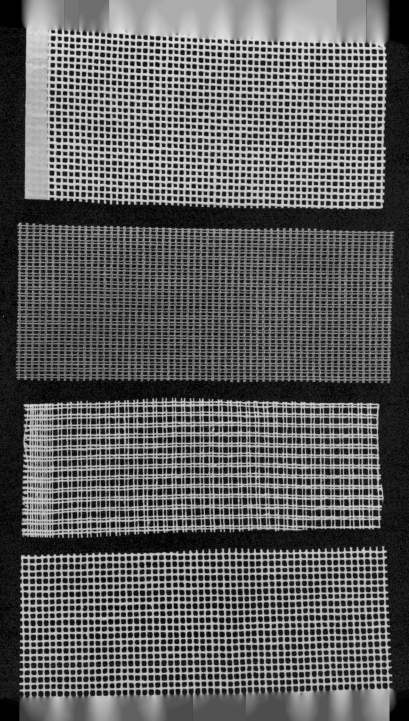

plain weave, a little stiffer and heavier of thread than the other canvases. It is very easy to paint on because of the heavy sizing, and it is very easy on the eyes because of the single-thread weave. You can tell a good quality of mono canvas by the highly polished thread used, and the low number of knots in the canvas. A poor quality of canvas becomes very limp, like paper, when wet. A good mono canvas is very durable.

Two-thread canvas is just what the name says. The two threads are woven evenly in pairs. The thread used is usually lighter than that used for mono canvas. It is not as easy to paint on and the price is much lower per yard. Rug canvas is a two-thread canvas, and the mesh is four or five to the inch. Penelope canvas is a specific type of two-thread canvas in which the warp threads are woven more closely together than the weft threads. The advantage of penelope is that you can get two mesh counts for the price of one: a ten-mesh penelope can be used as a twenty-mesh mono by spreading the pairs of mesh apart with your needle. This way the subject matter could be done at twenty mesh per inch and the background at ten mesh per inch, all on the same piece of work. Most stores carry 10/20 penelope, some carry 12/24 and a durable 7/14 mesh per inch.

Leno canvas is the latest arrival on the needlepoint market. It is made of a lighter thread than the other types of canvas and is more intricately woven. It is actually a two-thread canvas

The various canvases:
  mono canvas
  penelope
  two thread canvas
  leno canvas

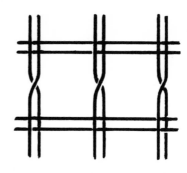

Leno Diagram

with warp and weft threads placed very close together. In addition, the pairs of warp threads are crossed or half-twisted in between each set of weft threads. The advantage of this is that the warp threads seem narrower, more like mono canvas, thereby making leno suitable for stitches that can only be done on mono. The intricate weave also has the advantage of two-thread canvas in that some stitches cannot be worked on mono canvas because of the looseness of the weave. The weave also makes the canvas less likely to ravel on a cut edge, a problem with other canvases. Leno is easy to paint on and silk screen.

Leno canvas has a more even mesh count than mono canvas. Though mono canvas may count fourteen mesh per inch warpwise, there is apt to be more or less than fourteen mesh to the inch weft-wise. This can produce a slight distortion in your design if you're counting it out from a graph design. This is one of the reasons why it is important to work canvas so that the warp threads run vertically as you work. This is easy to remember if you keep the selvage of the canvas always on the left side of your work. If you must cut a piece of canvas from the middle of the canvas, mark with a crayon or a dressmaker's chalk the direction of the warp. The uneven mesh count is also the reason why two pieces of canvas which are to be joined evenly side by side should be cut from the same piece of canvas, side by side if possible. This is vital when cutting the canvas for a pieced rug: it should be cut as it will lie on the floor.

Choose your canvas according to your durability requirements, the scale of the design you plan to use, and the amount of detail required. Obviously eighteen mesh will make available more mesh for detail than ten mesh, but eighteen mesh would not be appropriate for a rug in a ten-year-old boy's room. When you buy canvas, request a piece without knots or as few as possible. The knots are an inevitable part of weaving and cannot be totally avoided. Canvas should be cut evenly along one thread.

When planning your project, leave at least an inch and a half of bare canvas around the edge to make blocking and finishing easier. The cut edges of canvas should be treated to prevent ravelling and snagging of wool threads. You can hem the edges or cover them with masking tape, or sew on binding tape, or paint them with a liquid latex such as Rug-Sta (available at the hardware store). Even nail polish will work.

Wool

The important thing to consider in the choice of your wool is whether or not it covers the canvas adequately. Persian yarn and crewel wool are the choices of most needlepointers today. This is because these wools are fine enough to be used on high mesh count canvases but can be used multistrand on the lower meshes. Wools made for needlepoint should have a long smooth fiber and a fairly loose twist.

Persian yarn is made up of three threads of wool in one strand. You may use it full strand or separate it to use just one or two. It is sold by weight or by the strand. Each strand is about a yard and three-quarters long. It is the yarn most often found in custom kits.

Crewel wool is a two-ply fine wool sold by the strand or by weight, each strand about thirty inches long. It may be used single strand or as many as seven or eight per needle. Tapestry yarn is a heavier four-ply wool sold only by weight. It covers

13

ten mesh canvas well and, when doubled in the needle, some of the lower mesh canvases as well. There are several rya weight yarns available. They are coarser in texture than tapestry yarn but are close in actual size to it. Rug yarn is fatter still and a little softer. Some shops sell it by the strand but most by weight.

Cotton floss may be used on the finer mesh canvases and is very good for highlighting. Floss is multi-thread, four or six threads to the strand. Silk twist may be used in the same situations as cotton. It is more difficult to obtain and also more difficult to work with. Running each strand over a block of sewing wax will tame it somewhat. Knitting worsteds may be used for needlepoint but because they are essentially short-fibred yarns, they will not wear as well as yarns made for needlepoint. Chenile, raffia, or rayon novelty yarns may be used but should be limited to special effects and should be tested for color fastness before using.

Before buying any quantity of yarn for your needlepoint project do a small test swatch on the canvas you plan to use. Because some dyes are more caustic than others and some colors of wool are "fatter" than others, there are variations in the covering capabilities in the same brand of wool. No canvas should show through your stitches at all. If the wool is too thick for the canvas it will push or spread the mesh. When you are satisfied that the wool covers, adding or subtracting a thread to make it fit, only then should you invest in the project's wool. There is no uniformity of thickness in the several brands of Persian yarn currently on the market. Please test before using.

To estimate how much wool you will need for your project you may choose to take the easy way out and use the rule of

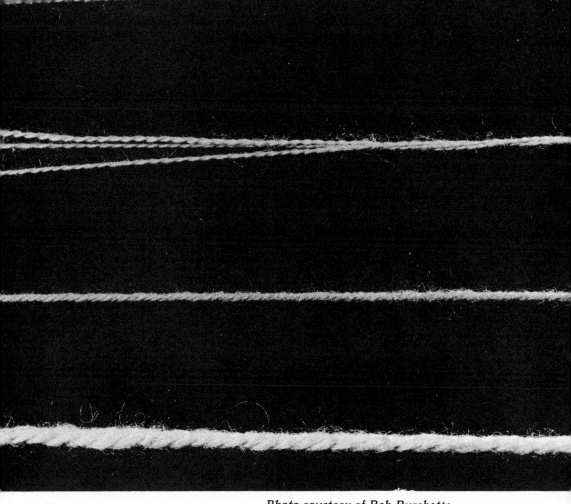

The various wools:
  crewel wool
  Persian wool
  tapestry wool
  rug wool

Photo courtesy of Bob Burchette

thumb the shops do. That is, if you are using Persian yarn. The shops figure that one full strand of Persian will cover one square inch of canvas in the customary needlepoint stitch, the half cross stitch. This rule applies for ten mesh to fourteen mesh canvases, and is a generous estimate to be on the safe side. For the larger mesh canvases, a little more than a strand is needed, a strand plus one quarter. For the finer canvases, less than a strand is needed. Remember that a strand is a generous yard and three quarters long.

If you want to figure out your own estimate, work a square inch of the stitch you plan to use with the wool and canvas of your choice. Measure each needleful of wool before you use it and subtract what is finally left in your needle when you are through. This gets complicated if you are using two threads of a three-thread strand. The answer to this is to do all your figuring on the basis of a full strand and then subtract a third of the final answer.

But to get on with the formula: Measure the area you wish to cover on your canvas by length and width. Multiply these numbers by each other. Multiply this total by the number of inches it takes to cover a square inch (this is why you made the little sample). Divide this total by thirty-six to convert back to yards or by sixty inches to figure the number of strands.

Needles

Needlepoint needles, also known as tapestry needles, are short and blunt. They range in size from numbers 24 to 14, even numbers only. The higher the number the needle is, the higher the number of mesh on which it will be used. For example, a number 18 needle is right for ten mesh mono canvas.

16

There is a super-large size made for rug canvas. It is three inches long. The needle size is proper if the canvas threads are not moved when the threaded needle is stabbed through the canvas.

Starting Pointers

There are two ways of threading a needle. One is to fold the wool and, squeezing it between the thumb and forefinger, thrust the bend of the fold through the eye of the needle. Pull it through, making sure all fibers have squeezed through too. The other way is to trim the end of the wool and, again squeezing it between the forefinger and—this time—the thumb nail (as close as possible to the wool end), force it through the eye of the needle. This method is advisable when your needle eye is a little small for the amount of wool passing through it.

Threading Needle

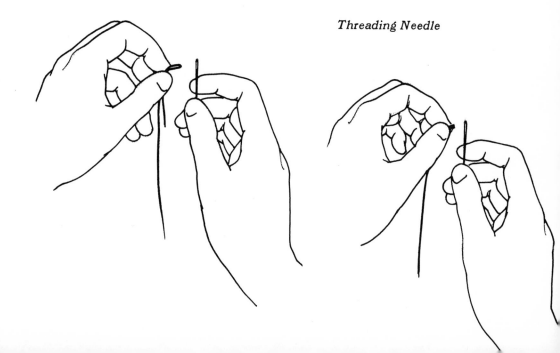

The finer the needle you are using, the shorter should be the thread. A size 22 needle would carry a strand of wool only about fourteen inches long. An 18 needle would carry no more than twenty inches of wool. The reason for such brevity is that as the wool passes through the canvas, some fibers come loose and fall off. Thus the end of the thread will be thinner than in the beginning, making for uneven-looking stitches. Cut your wool to appropriate lengths for each project. With a scrap strand, tie each bundle loosely so that you can draw out a strand at a time without having a tangled mess.

Scrolling

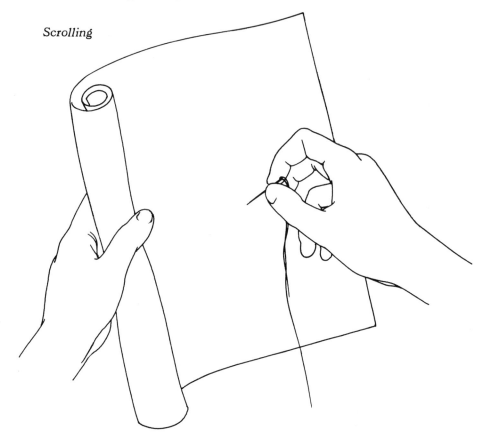

One habit that will guarantee more even-looking stitches is to twirl the needle between your fingers as you work. This helps to keep the wool threads aligned and not twisted too tightly, thereby letting the wool lie flatter on the canvas. To make the canvas more comfortable to hold as you work, roll it as you would a scroll. Hold the canvas by the roll in your left hand (or right hand if you are left-handed). If you are left-handed, work the following stitch diagrams with the book upside down.

To start your first thread, put the needle in the canvas in the path of the stitches you expect to work first. (Remember, the selvage of the canvas should be on your left.) Allow an inch-long tag of wool to remain on the face of the canvas. If you like to knot your thread, do so, but let the knot lie on the face of the canvas. Your stitches will catch up the wool on the back of the canvas as you work, thereby securing it. A little conscious effort to do this at first is not a bad idea. Snip off the tag or knot when your stitches come to it.

When you come to the end of the thread, you may finish it off either by running it through the backs of nearby completed stitches for an inch; or by finishing the way you started. Simply

How to Start Thread

How to Finish Thread

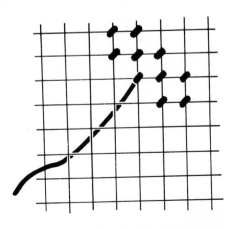

leave a tag of wool on the face of the canvas about three quarters of an inch away from your last stitch, but in the path of the next needleful of stitches. When you eventually progress to the tag, you will have caught up the wool on the back of the canvas with your ongoing work. Snip off the tag as before. This method prevents the very slight long lumps on the face of the work caused by running in the backs of the stitches to finish.

Keep the back of your work as neat of stray tag ends as you can. If left, they have an annoying habit of traveling to the surface of the canvas with nearby stitches.

This amusing elephant pillow was designed by Carol and Harold Sherley of The Knittery, San Francisco, California. It combines seven canvas stitches and one crewel stitch. Note the turkey work fringe on the elephant's blanket.

The reverse mirror image pillow was designed by Mrs. Ruth Klausmeyer of Cincinnati, Ohio, in shades of gold and cream.

The Half Cross Stitch

The basic needlepoint stitch is known by several names and there are three different ways of working it. A whole cross stitch consists of two stitches or strokes worked over one intersection of canvas threads. Therefore, if only one stroke is used, it is half of a cross stitch, hence the name. The half cross stitch may be worked in the continental stitch, the basket weave stitch, or in quickpoint.

21

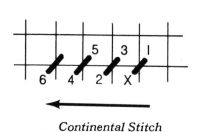

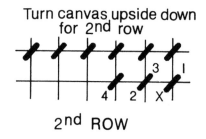

2nd ROW

Continental Stitch

THE CONTINENTAL STITCH should be used for detail work only. It has one unfortunate trait: it slants or biases the canvas when worked in any quantity. The canvas is more or less "tied" into the slanting position by the nature of the stitch. You can see that large areas of the stitch would be unwise, especially as a background stitch. The use of an embroidery frame will correct the situation; however, the beauty of the stitch is that it can be worked in one thrust of the needle. The use of a frame will require two stabs of the needle per stitch. Those who use graph patterns for their designs usually rely on the continental stitch for the subject matter, but not for the background.

To start the stitch, bring the needle up from the back of the canvas at X. Insert the needle at 1 and out at 2. Do this in one stroke. Pull the wool through. The wool following the needle will neatly cover the intersection of the canvas threads, making your first stitch. The next stitch starts at 3 and is stroked through to 4 and so on across the canvas. The continental stitch is always worked from right to left. When you come to the end of a row, turn the canvas upside down and start again in the empty row of mesh underneath. Start at X again.

22

The continental stitch, front on the right, the back on the left

THE BASKET WEAVE STITCH is the "professional's" stitch. It should be used wherever possible because it has less tendency to bias the canvas than the other two half cross stitches. It can be worked back and forth diagonally without having to turn the canvas around as one does with the continental. It is called the basket weave stitch because it looks like basket weave on the back of the canvas.

Starting in the upper-right-hand corner of your canvas (lower-left for left-handers), thrust the needle through the canvas at X, insert it at 1 and out again at 2. Insert the needle at 3, under two canvas threads and out at 4, in at 5 and out at 6. Yes, you did just work a continental stitch—that is how you finish a row and turn around with the basket weave stitch. All of these stitches should have been worked with one thrust of the needle on the face of the canvas. Insert the needle at 7 and down to 8 under two threads of the canvas. You always go under two threads of canvas to make a basket weave half cross stitch. You always point the needle toward your stomach when you are working a down row, and always point the needle toward your other hand when working an up row. This applies to left-handers too.

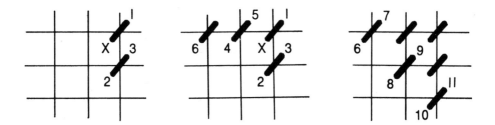

Basket Weave Stitch

If you must stop working suddenly to answer the phone, leave your needle pointing in the direction you were working. This is very important if you are at the end of a row. If you mix the up and down sequence of rows it will create a diagonal ridge in your work. Of course, you can tell the direction of your stitches by examining the back of the canvas, but the pointing needle is simpler.

The basket weave stitch, front on the right, the back on the left

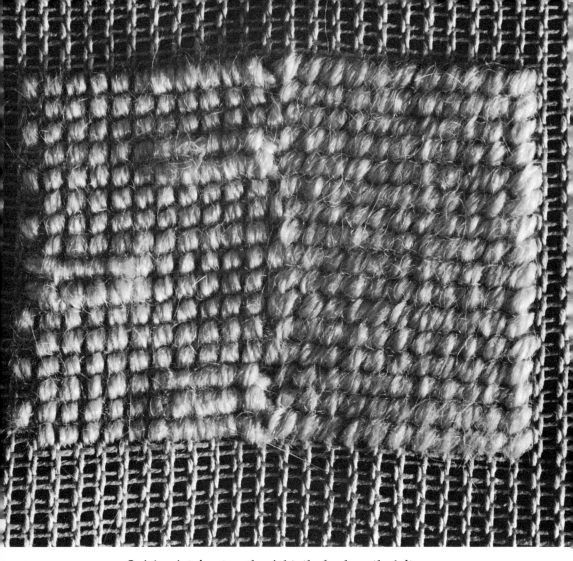

Quick point, front on the right, the back on the left

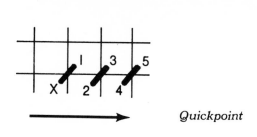

Quickpoint

Turn canvas upside down
for 2nd row

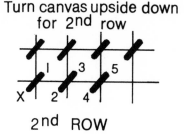

2nd ROW

THE QUICKPOINT STITCH has two disadvantages. The first is that it cannot be worked on mono canvas. It slips along the weft canvas threads and won't stay in its place. The other disadvantage is that it biases the canvas quite badly. The good side of the picture is that the stitch is very easy to do. It is suitable for teaching to small children to whom you can reteach the more complicated and usable stitches later on.

The stitch is worked from left to right. Bring the needle to the face of the canvas at **X**, go in again at 1, out at 2 in one stroke of the needle. Continue on to 3-4, 5-6, and so on. At the end of the row turn the canvas upside down and work the next row underneath.

The little girl was designd and worked by Mrs. Philip Weymouth, Jr. of Creative Critters, Wilmington, Delaware. Her back has been worked in needlepoint too; the colors are pink, purple, orange and yellow. French knots form the eyes and the centers of the flowers.

Chapter Two

Design

THERE is no great mystery to needlepoint design; however, there are a few tricks of the trade. The novice designer would do well to start off with simple designs, leaving out as much detail as possible. With experience you will learn to scale your design to the size canvas you are using. You will see that flat strong colors will be most effective on a large mesh rug canvas, a more subtle design would go on ten mesh canvas, and even more intricacy of design and color would fit eighteen mesh canvas.

There are many excellent design books available for inspiration. Your public library can help you there, and Dover Publications have some fine ones in paperback. Near Eastern and Oriental art books have wonderful ideas to adapt, as do porcelain and textile books. Coloring books are excellent sources of design, as are most children's books. If you want to do a more abstract design, cut out of construction paper various shapes. They could be leaves, fruit, even fish. Move the shapes around until the placement pleases you. Paste the shapes in place, and there you have your original design.

Wallpaper sample books contain great repeat patterns. Nursery catalogues contain excellent design ideas in their color photographs. Color photographs in magazines are helpful in learning how to shade. With a pencil you can outline the shading and highlights very easily.

If your design is too small for the space you wish to fill, it can be enlarged photographically, or at home. Sketch or trace your design, take it to a photographer for a photostatic enlargement. It can be done to your exact measurements, and is relatively inexpensive to do.

If you would rather enlarge your design yourself, rule lines horizontally and vertically over your tracing. On another sheet of paper rule out the size you want the design to be and fill that space with the same number of lines as there are to your design. Of course, they will be further apart. Starting at the center of the design, draw in the contents of each square as shown in the diagram.

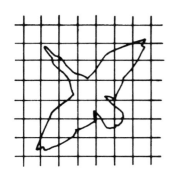

Enlarging Design

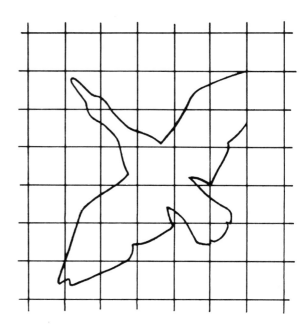

Sally Pierson designed the Sun King for the Nantucket Needleworks of Nantucket, Massachusetts. The colors are yellow, pink and fuchsia, with a white background.

Color

Simplicity is the best policy when it comes to color for your first project. If you lack confidence in your color selection put the color wheel to work for you. The safest color scheme is a monochromatic one, that is, several shades of one color, such as blue ranging from navy blue to pale blue. Colors opposite each other on the color wheel make up a complementary scheme. For instance, use blue and orange, perhaps adding shades of one or the other.

31

A triadic scheme calls for three colors all at opposite points of a triangle on the color wheel, for instance, yellow, blue, and red. The most subtle schemes are the analogous, that is, colors side by side on the color wheel, such as yellow, chartreuse, and green. Black, white, brown, and gray are not included on most color wheels. Brown and gray are not included because the former is a combination of two colors present, and the latter is an addition of black to other colors. Black, white, and gray will join practically any color scheme comfortably. Brown should be added with care. Gray is a good unifying color. It is a great color to use when you don't want to disrupt a pretty color balance with another color of equal value.

Black placed next to a very bright color will serve to focus attention on it. Two colors used in a small checkered pattern will blend at a distance and will produce another color entirely. For instance, red and green checks will produce a brown tone. Warm colors will come toward you and cold colors will recede. Keep this in mind in choosing colors for your subject matter. You don't want your background color to dominate. A light color will make a chair seat seem higher, a dark color lower. Using a color twice, or two shades of the same color on a canvas, gives a design a very cohesive look.

A group of bright colors, such as fiery orange, chrome yellow, and bright green, will cancel each other out, none of them being dominant. Thus, if you want one color to stand out, team it with quieter mates, for instance, chrome yellow with two shades of hyacinth. Do not be afraid to choose very vivid colors for your needlepoint. Somehow when wool colors are stitched over canvas they seem to fade out. A color that looks zowie on the shop counter will tame down considerably on the canvas.

32

You must decide whether to outline your subject matter or have hard edge meet hard edge. Part of this decision may be made for you by your choice of design. Outlining your design is a good way to learn a little about shading. Try a shade lighter or darker than the mass you are outlining. As you work your design you will soon see that a few more stitches here or there would give added form and contour.

Remember that there is only one sun in the sky, so keep any shading you do consistently on the same side of all subjects. Light colors go toward the top on foliage, darker colors on the bottom to show shade. Foreground colors should be brighter. Grayer hues show distance.

Color Wheel

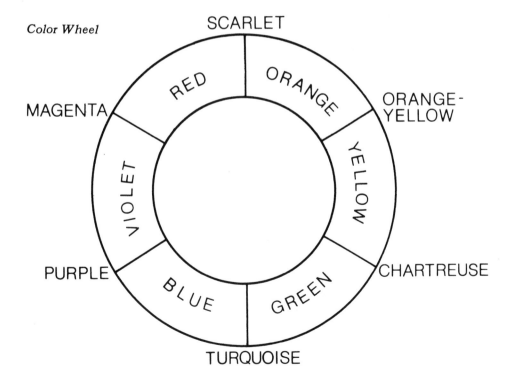

If you want shading to delineate an object such as one flower petal against another, skip one or two shades on the wool card. This is especially true with light colors, where quite a contrast is needed. Because of the contrasts needed, you will find that you cannot accurately duplicate colors as they are in the original. Don't worry. This is one place where accuracy is not important; it is the effect that counts.

Techniques

Having decided on your design and colors, it is now time to determine which medium to use to apply that design to the canvas. Scale is an important factor in the choice of the medium. Certain media just will not do for fine work. To help you decide, lay a piece of canvas of the mesh you plan to use over your design. You will see at a glance how well your design will work on the canvas, just how much painstaking detail will be needed or not needed as the case may be.

There are five ways of applying a design to canvas. They are graph paper, which is suitable for small motifs, borders, or repeats; transfer and crayon, which are suitable for large masses and no detail; paint, right for more detailed projects and shading; and silk screen, strictly a professional's method.

Translating into Graph

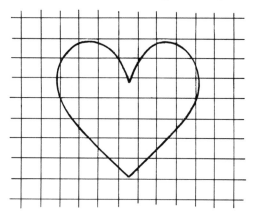 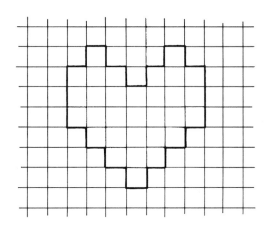

GRAPH PAPER is more a means than an application. Graph paper with ten squares to the inch is easy to work with. Draw your design on the paper and then block it out as shown in the diagram. You must make a decision on each square, whether to assign that square to the subject or the background. A good rule of thumb to follow is that if more than two-thirds of the square falls on the side of the subject, give that square to the subject. If more than two-thirds falls on the side of the background, that square goes to the background. Counting each square of the graph paper as one stitch, you count squares and work the requisite number of stitches. Each graph square counts as one intersection of the canvas.

A problem that arises in graph design arises in other methods too, and should be mentioned here. That is, the dot-dot effect. Single diagonal lines to the left create the dot-dot effect because the stitches don't touch head to tail the way they do to the right. There are two ways of compensating for this situation. The first way is to go ahead and design your single line of stitches to the left (the stem of a flower for instance, or a ski pole). Then when you stitch, work that single line in cross stitch with the top stroke slanting in the same direction as the rest of the stitches. The bottom strokes will connect, head to tail, and create a solid line for you. The other way to treat the problem is to design a double line of stitches, thus avoiding the situation all together.

Dot—Dot

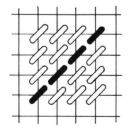 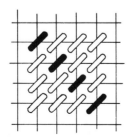 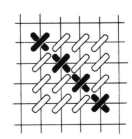

A small design "graphed" out

The same design worked on canvas

Another thing to consider while you are applying your design is space for fancy stitches. If you plan to use any fancy stitches, check to see how many mesh they need per stitch. For instance, the Smyrna cross stitch needs two by two mesh. The area in which this stitch would go should have an even rather than an odd number of mesh to fit properly.

AN IRON-ON TRANSFER is the next method of applying designs to canvas. This technique may be used two ways. After applying the transfer to the canvas, and with the original drawing nearby to follow for colors, you could start to stitch right away without painting at all. Or, using the transferred design rather like a coloring book outline, you can paint in the colors. If the transfer medium color is too bright, paint right over it, covering the outline. This is important because bright colors underneath your wool stitches will "shine" right through lighter color wools.

A disadvantage of using transfers is that it is not very precise. Since the design is not graphed out so to speak, you will have to make the subject-background decision as you stitch or paint.

To make a transfer you will need tracing layout paper. It is sold at art supply stores. There are three media to choose from to actually make the transfer. The first is, of course, transfer pencil. The British make a very fine one. Two good brands available in the United States are an Eberhard Faber Potent Copying Hectograph pencil and a Magic Transfer pencil. They are meant for crewel transfer really, are quite inexpensive, and may be bought at a needlework shop. The pencils come in two colors, a bright fuchsia and green. The green is preferable because it will not "shine" through quite as brightly as the fuchsia.

Another medium is embroidery paints such as Deco-Write or Artex. The former is available at craft supply shops and comes in twenty-six colors. You could outline in the colors of the wools you plan to use. Don't let the paint line become too thin or nothing will transfer.

The third medium is oil paints used without a thinner and applied with a fine brush. This is a slow method because the paint must dry twice, once after applying to the layout paper and again after the iron melts it on the canvas.

Trace your design on the layout paper. Turn the paper over so that the transfer will face the same direction as the original. Pencil over the tracing if you need to make it easier to see, otherwise apply your transfer medium to the design outline. On a drawing board large enough to accommodate the whole transfer, tack your piece of canvas. Lay the transfer face down on the board. Line up any straight lines in the transfer with the threads of the canvas. Using a hot steam iron press the transfer, making sure you cover all areas of the design. Really press down on the iron, but don't scorch the paper.

THE CRAYON METHOD is well suited for children's projects because the medium is readily available and not too messy. Only very simple designs are appropriate for this method. Using tracing paper or layout paper and a felt-tip pen trace your design or, as it is known in the needlepoint business, cartoon. Tack your cartoon to a drawing board and then tack your canvas over it. Line up the canvas threads so that they are quite straight with the edge of the paper. This seems to be an odd thing to suggest, but some canvas, particularly mono canvas, has a certain amount of sway in the middle of the width of canvas. This sway or curve could do nasty things to a straight Mondrian type of design.

Crayon right on the canvas, using all the colors you need. Outline if you wish or color in all the way. When you are finished, remove the canvas from the board and lay it out on a layer of paper toweling on an ironing board. Cover the canvas with another layer of paper toweling. With a warm iron quickly swish across the design area. The purpose of the paper towel sandwich is to remove any excess wax from the canvas so that it won't crumble into the wool. All the wax should not be removed or it will take all the color too.

PAINT is the most professional method of applying a design to canvas. Again, a tracing of your design must be made on layout paper using a felt-tip pen so that the design will show clearly

Mr. A. Alvis Layne of Washington, D.C. worked the belt for his daughter-in-law, Mrs. Patricia R. Layne. It was designed by Desirée.

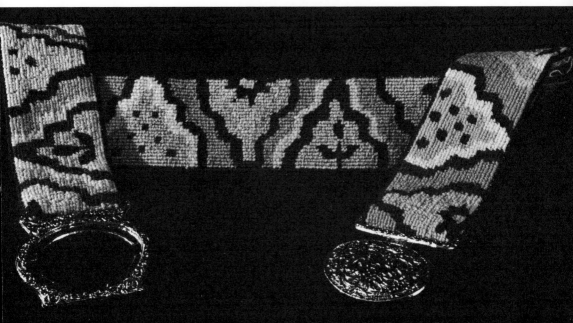

through the canvas. The finished cartoon (outline only is necessary) should be tacked to a drawing board and the canvas lined up on the sides and then tacked down too. Incidentally, if your design is very symmetrical, some counting of mesh may be required as you paint, so that both sides will be equal. Use a dressmakers chalk to mark your counting; can be brushed off later.

Most people use acrylic paints nowadays rather than oil paints. Acrylics are quick drying (three or four hours) and safer to mix (water rather than turpentine). Enough water should be added so that the paint is the consistency of canned cream. If it is too thin, the canvas thread acts as a wick and the color runs along the thread. If it is too thick, the mesh are clogged and will have to be poked out with a needle to take a stitch. Fine sable brushes are recommended.

The big secret in applying color to canvas, whether by crayon or paint, is this: An intersection of canvas threads can hold only one color. A well-painted canvas is one where you can see without straining exactly which color will be stitched over each intersection. You cannot sketch on canvas if you want to work it easily and happily.

If you wish, polymer gloss medium may be added to the acrylics to give the finished project a more professional look. If your canvas looks undersized (the stiffening), a coat of gloss medium will make it more paintable. It is recommended that gloss medium be painted over finished dry canvases, whether crayoned, transferred, or painted. A product like Blair Spray Clear Protective Coating or Devoe Clear Acrylic Plastic Spray will work as well. The reason for this final coat is to protect the media from cleaning fluid and Scotch-Gard, both of which will make the media run if enough is applied.

Oil paints should be the same consistency as acrylics for applying to canvas. To hasten drying, a very few drops of Japan dryer may be added to each color. This will darken the colors somewhat but not enough to matter. Oil paints will dry in a couple of days without Japan dryer, in about twenty-four hours with.

Magic markers can be used on canvas, but only after you have tested them thoroughly. Many brands of marker say right on the tube that they are waterproof, but they are not telling the truth. Test on a scrap of canvas every color you plan to use. Lay a wet paper towel over your marked canvas, press it down with your hand, and then leave it for half an hour. If any of the colors run, discard them. The reason for such stern treatment is that in the blocking process the canvas is either dampened or outright wet. The runny markers will bleed their colors into surrounding wools, ruining the canvas. Dry cleaning will not help. Ball-point pens have the same effect when wet. Please test any marker pens before using. Be sure if you do use markers that you paint or spray the canvas with gloss medium or acrylic spray.

The advantage of a painted canvas is that less white canvas shows through if your stitches are a little thin in places. The disadvantage is that, if there are large areas of dark color to work over, it is hard to see the canvas mesh. You will have to decide for yourself how much this bothers you.

SILK SCREEN is a special technique unto itself and is too complicated to describe in a book of this scope. Professional studios with a need to reproduce a design one hundred times would find this method useful and economical.

41

Mrs. S. Clark Woodard of Washington, D.C., inherited a set of canvases designed and worked by her grandmother who based them on Gustave Doré's Les Fables de La Fontaine. Shown here are the illustrations from Doré's book and Madame Rougny's interpretation of it.

The seashore arrangement by James DeVries was designed for the Nantucket Needleworks of Nantucket, Massachusetts. It is in shades of blue, gray, and beige.

Chapter Three

The Fancy Stitches

EACH of the fancy stitches has its own little quirks and foibles. Some will work only on leno and mono canvases and others only on two-thread canvases. Those included here are fairly reliable as far as not biasing the canvas too much. If they do, a frame is recommended. Care must be taken in choosing fancy stitches so that the proportion of the stitch will be appropriate to the space allotted for it. As a generalization, unsafe as they are, fancy stitches are not effective on mesh finer than fourteen per inch. The stitches become miniaturized to such an extent that the texture factor is lost. The obvious exception, of course, is bargello. It looks great on even twenty-four mesh to the inch.

It is not possible to make a smooth curve in needlepoint because of the nature of the material it is worked on. Edges appear to be jagged. This jagged effect is accentuated by textured stitches. If you want to minimize this irregularity, don't use fancy stitches for the background if the subject matter is worked in half cross stitch. Remember that light colors show texture better than dark colors. If you have space in the area allotted that will not take a complete fancy stitch, just fill it in with half cross stitches in the same color. Of course, some of the fancy stitches will half very nicely and no problem arises.

Work your fancy stitches right along with your half cross stitches unless you know that a certain stitch will bias the canvas. In that case save that stitch area until last. Then mount your canvas in a frame and work your biasing stitch. You may find that you like working with a frame; using one does seem to make all stitches look more uniform.

To mount your canvas into a rectangular scroll frame, pin or sew your canvas to the tape attached to the long bars. Turn the long bars (first loosening the screws) until the canvas is where you need to work it. Attach a thread of carpet thread to the side bar and lash the canvas to the side bars on both sides. The canvas should be taut in the frame. If you need to move the canvas along to work another area, cut the carpet threads and turn the long bars to the new location. Re-lash the sides to make the canvas taut again.

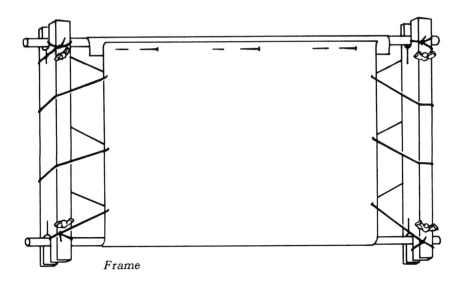

Frame

Some of the following stitches are customarily diagrammed covering many more mesh than shown here. To indicate that they have been reduced in size, "modified" has been added in parentheses. Hopefully the stitches will be more usable in their reduced state. The stitches were chosen for either their versatility or their usefulness. But this is only a sample. There are over a hundred more for you to try.

The little boudoir rug with the tassel border was designed and worked by Martha White Quentin of Art Needlework of Georgia in Atlanta, Georgia. The background is pink, the border green and the fans various pale pastels.

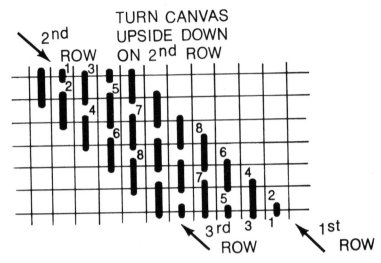

Brick Stitch

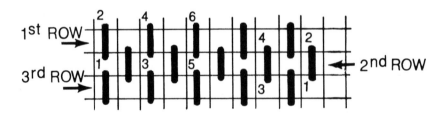

THE BRICK STITCH is a simple upright stitch worked over two mesh. It is an excellent background stitch giving a little more texture than the half cross stitch. Because it is a small stitch it can be worked in the interstices of a complicated design. To give a clean edge to the stitch on a horizontal row, just work upright stitches over one mesh. More strands of wool per needle are

48

needed to cover the canvas than with the half cross stitch on the same canvas. The stitch should be worked only on mono canvas and leno canvas. The double warp threads of penelope and two-thread canvas will show between the stitches if it is worked on these canvases. This is true of all upright stitches on two-thread canvas.

The brick stitch may be worked two ways. The *first way* is just to cover ground. It is more economical of wool than the other way. Be sure that your stitch tension is even, otherwise a diagonal ridge will result.

The *second way* provides a heavier backing on the back of the canvas. This is important if you are combining the brick stitch and another heavily backed stitch (such as the basket weave stitch) in a rug or wall hanging. Canvas will ripple if a lightly backed stitch is worked next to a heavily backed stitch. You can see the problem which would be created if the lightly backed stitch were on the border of a rug.

The brick stitch

BARGELLO is a long upright stitch worked in progressive steps in progressive shades of wool to form a pattern which repeats itself. The stitch may cover from three to six or more mesh. The next stitch beside it will be the same length but two or three mesh below it. Thus you may have a combination such as four mesh for each stitch and two mesh down (or up) for the next stitch. This is known as a four-two combination and is the most commonly used. The second number in the combination is sometimes called a step. That means that the four mesh upright stitch steps up (or down) two mesh for the next stitch.

The next row follows the pattern set up by the first. To show off the pattern, each row is worked in a repeating series of colors or shades of colors. Some patterns consist of two or three colors in ascending graduations of shades. Some patterns form sharp peaks, diamonds within diamonds, even fish scales. If the pattern is a peaked one, there is usually a center peak with the left side

Bargello   of the pattern being a mirror image of the right side.

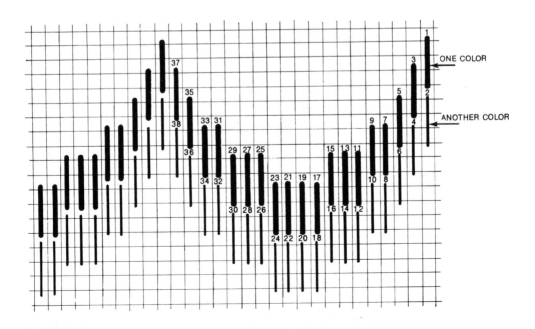

The accompanying diagram is a very simple example of bargello or, as it is also known, Florentine embroidery. Bargello can be worked only on mono and leno canvas. Fold your canvas in half to find the exact center two mesh to start. Mark the center with dressmaker's chalk or run a basting thread along the length of the center mesh. You need to find the exact center so that the pattern will come out evenly on both sides.

Remember that with this stitch you count the *holes* between the mesh horizontally to plot the pattern across the canvas. You count the *canvas threads* vertically to compute the length of each stitch. Again, you will have to experiment to see how much wool is needed in your needle, but expect to use a good third more.

Work the first row in your lightest or darkest shade. Work the second row directly underneath it. Get in the habit of twirling your needle to untwist the wool. The stitches should lie flat to cover. If canvas shows through between rows, add more wool in your needle. Work the stitches as the numbers in the diagram show it; wool likes to coil around and around. If the wool fibers are bent (as shown in the diagram), they will not lie flat but will flop over sideways giving a poor-looking stitch. Varying the way of stitching, from coiling to bending, will cause the canvas to ripple like corduroy. The ripple will never block out.

A good way to keep your various shades of wool in order and tidy while you are working bargello is to snap them into a strip of Conso's snap tape. It is meant for upholstery and consists of two strips of tape with snaps every inch or so. Just insert your various shades between the snaps.

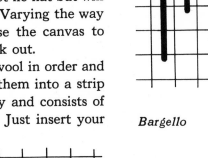

Bargello

Wool Bent

Bargello

Parisian Embroidery

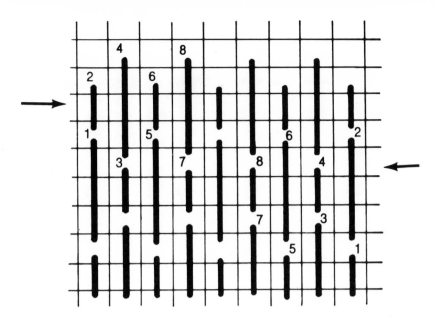

Parisian embroidery

PARISIAN EMBROIDERY is a combination of the two foregoing stitches, a short upright stitch and a long one. The pattern of the stitch is strong enough that it looks well in one color; however, it is very attractive worked in rows of two colors. More wool is needed in your needle than for the half cross stitch on the same canvas. If the stitch is worked in two colors, you may find that you need more wool in your needle with one color than the other. Work only on mono canvas and leno canvas.

The wool should be kept untwisted as you work so that the stitches will lie flat. This stitch does bias the canvas a little, for though the front of the stitch is straight up, the back of the stitch is slanted. If worked over a large area a frame would be helpful. Parisian embroidery covers an area quickly and has a firm backing. It fits in odd spaces because it quarters and halves easily. It can be worked from either right or left.

53

The enlarged Parisian embroidery stitch   Photo courtesy of Hugh Grubb

ENLARGED PARISIAN EMBROIDERY is a sturdy stitch with a strong pattern to it. It may be worked in one color, or with the tie-down stitch in another color, or in alternating colors. You will need about a third more wool in your needle than you would for the half cross stitch on the same canvas. It can be worked on mono, leno and penelope canvases, but not on two thread, the stitch halves easily thus fitting odd sized spaces. It can be worked in either direction, just keep the long stitches flat and untwisted.

Both the in and out strokes of the tie-down stitch (7-8) are made from the same hole in the canvas. The stitch does bias the canvas a little. A frame is recommended if it is to be worked over a large area. It has a very firm backing.

Enlarged Parisian Embroidery

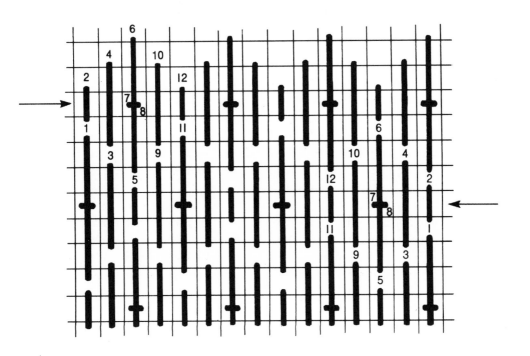

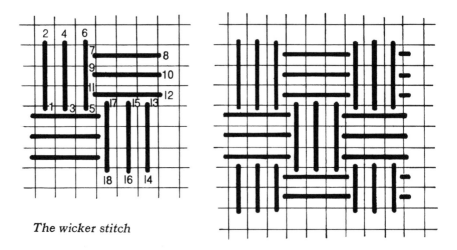

The wicker stitch

THE WICKER STITCH has the look of a rough wicker or split wood basket. It covers the canvas quickly and does not bias the canvas. You must be consistent in the way you stitch it, as you are with bargello. Either coil the wool around the canvas mesh or bend the wool, but not both on the same canvas. Bulges and ripples will be the result if you do. No extra wool is needed in the needle for this stitch.

As you work each set of three stitches, it is a good idea to hold back with your thumb the last stitch of the last set worked. This is so that you may see the mesh to work from. The wicker stitch will halve and quarter well to fit odd spaces. An outside outline of half cross stitch is recommended to make the edge of the stitch area a little more sharp looking. Because it is composed of upright stitches, this stitch should be worked on leno and mono canvas only.

56

Wicker Stitch

Upright Cross Stitch

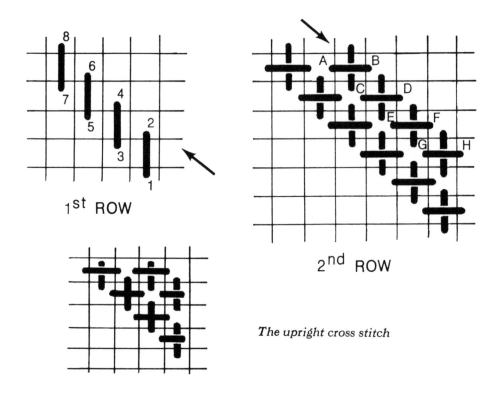

1ˢᵗ ROW

2ⁿᵈ ROW

The upright cross stitch

THE UPRIGHT CROSS STITCH is a pair of crossed brick stitches. It makes a dandy background stitch, does not bias the canvas much, and has a firm backing. You may need less wool in your needle than you would for the half cross stitch on the same canvas. The stitch may be worked on penelope canvas if you think it covers well enough, but it is really best on leno and mono canvas. Work the vertical stitches in one trip up the canvas and then cross them horizontally in one trip back down. Diagram 3 shows how to halve the stitches.

THE DIAGONAL FRENCH STITCH is a combination of a long upright stitch and a short upright stitch crossed. It will use about as much wool as the half cross stitch on the same kind of canvas. The stitch does not bias the canvas and has a firm backing. Work a row of long cross stitches and then cross them with the short horizontal stitches. Try working every other horizontal row of stitches in a different color than the background. The stroking of this stitch is very similar to the upright cross but the result is quite different. Diagram 3 shows how to halve the stitch. The stitch can be done on leno, mono, and penelope canvas, but does not cover well on two thread.

Diagonal French Stitch

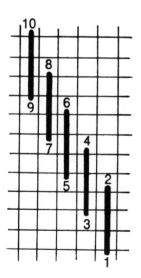 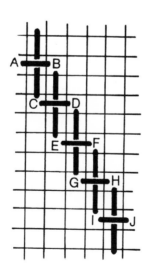 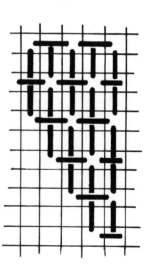

The diagonal French stitch

The cross stitch

THE CROSS STITCH is a more textured stitch than the half cross stitch, and can be used in the same situations. It makes a very subtle background stitch. It produces a firm backing and causes very little bias to the canvas. Less wool is needed in the needle than with the half cross stitch on the same type of canvas.

The diagrammed stroking of the stitch will hopefully correct the "wrapped" look the cross stitch often has. The stitch is completed in one trip across the canvas. The "wrapped" look occurs when one complete row of half cross stitch is worked across the canvas and then the top row of stitches is worked back over it. If the diagrammed stroking makes the stitches look as if they are running together, you are either working it too tightly, or you are nibbling into the stitch just completed with your needle.

One must turn the canvas around at the end of each row because it can only be worked from right to left (left to right for left-handers). The cross stitch prefers a two-thread canvas but can be worked *this* way on mono canvas even over one intersection of mesh.

If the canvas shows when the cross stitch is worked over two mesh each way, try tramé underneath. Ordinarily tramé is worked beneath a pair of weft threads on penelope to show the design, but it can also be used to help cover the canvas. Tramé can be laid between two threads of mono canvas, leno canvas, or two-thread canvas. It should be stitched irregularly to avoid a sequence of tell-tale ridges. Use the same color wool as the top stitching. Fasten the beginning of the tramé wool in the backs of nearby completed stitches and finish the same way.

Cross Stitch

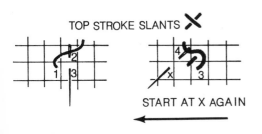

TOP STROKE SLANTS ✗

START AT X AGAIN

←

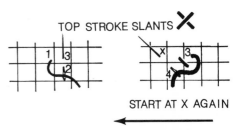

TOP STROKE SLANTS ✗

START AT X AGAIN

←

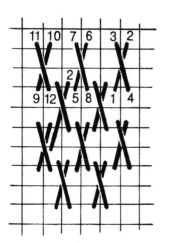 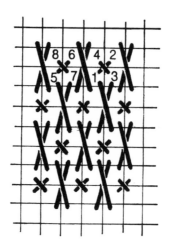 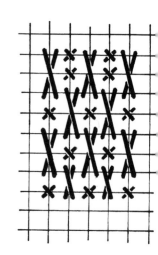

Double Stitch

THE DOUBLE STITCH combines a small cross stitch with a very long cross stitch. This stitch is difficult to work on a finer mesh canvas than ten mesh per inch. Since it has a rather coarse look anyway, the effect is lost on a small scale. It has a distinct woven look which can be enhanced by making the small cross stitch a different color than the long crosses. The stitch provides a reasonably firm backing and biases the canvas very little. It does not work well on mono canvas.

More wool will be needed in the needle than usual. Keep your wool untwisted as you work and your tension loose. Work the long crosses first, then the small ones. Cross all the stitches in the same direction. Fill in at the start and again at the finish with an extra row of small cross stitches. Diagram 3 shows how to halve the stitch.

The double stitch

The Smyrna cross stitch

Smyrna Cross Stitch

THE SMYRNA CROSS STITCH is a very textured stitch but at the same time presents a neat appearance. It is quite popular as a border stitch and for rugs. The same amount of wool is needed in your needle as for the half cross stitch. The wool must fit the canvas just right so that no canvas threads show between the stitches. It should have a chubby look on the canvas, not thin and anemic. The Smyrna cross stitch works well on any type of canvas.

The stitch does not halve well, therefore the space planned for it must be divisible by two so that each stitch can be complete. You can work the stitch all at once or the bottom crosses first, then the top crosses. Just make sure that the top strokes are all worked in the same direction.

Triple Cross Stitch

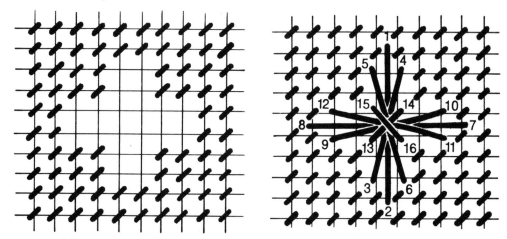

THE TRIPLE CROSS STITCH makes a very splashy showing as a display stitch. It is not meant to be joined closely to others of its kind. The background for the stitch must be worked first because the two top strokes of the triple cross stitch are worked right into it.

Allot a Greek-cross-shaped space six mesh by six by two wide for each triple cross stitch. Mark it in dressmaker's chalk, then work the half cross stitch all around it. Then work the long stitches right into the first row of the backgrounding half cross stitches. Work the smallest cross stitch last. If you do a field of these stitches, make sure the top stitches all slant in the same direction.

You will need the same amount of wool in your needle for the triple cross stitch as you do for the half cross background. Any canvas will do.

The triple cross stitch   *Photo courtesy of Hugh Grubb*

THE KNIT STITCH (or Kalem stitch) is another excellent background stitch which will work on any canvas. It takes a little less wool in your needle than the half cross stitch on the same canvas. It provides a reasonably firm backing and will bias the canvas only if worked tightly. Work a half cross stitch in the opposite direction at the beginning and end of each row. This makes for a neater edge.

The knit stitch may be worked horizontally or vertically, whichever is the most comfortable for you. The stitch should be stroked in and out with one thrust, like the continental stitch (the knit stitch is the continental stitch worked wrong side out).

Knit Stitch

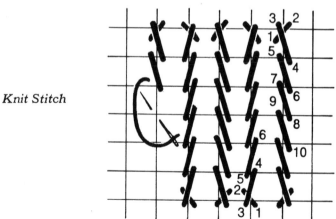

The knit stitch

The oblique Slav stitch

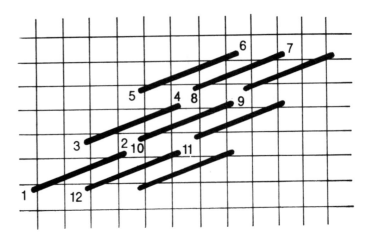

Oblique Slav Stitch

THE OBLIQUE SLAV STITCH is a good stitch for geometric designs where the space can be planned for it. It is not very suitable for figurative designs because it does not halve well. On the good side of the ledger, it does work on any canvas. The key to success with this stitch is to have enough wool in your needle to really cover the canvas. It uses much more than the half cross stitch would on the same canvas.

If you like geometric designs, this is a great stitch to experiment with. Covering as many mesh as it does per stitch it works up very quickly. It does not bias the canvas unless a large area is worked with all the stitches slanting in the same direction.

THE LEAF STITCH (modified) is a very versatile stitch, useful as a background stitch as well as for borders. It may be stitched in one solid color or three or four. The leaf stitch combines nicely with many fancy stitches but especially the brick stitch. The wool must fit the canvas just right with this stitch or the canvas will show. Experiment to see how much you will need to cover. Leno and mono canvases are the best ones to use, but penelope will do if the wool fits just right. The leaf stitch does not bias the canvas at all. Keep twirling the needle to keep the wool untwisted so the stitches will lie flat.

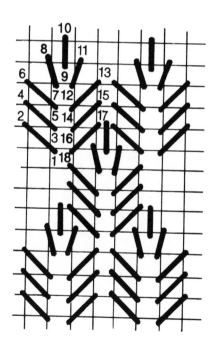

Leaf Stitch

The leaf stitch

The mosaic stitch

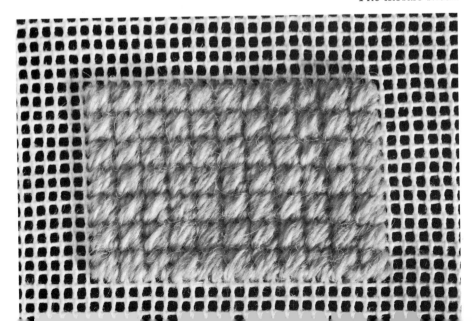

THE MOSAIC STITCH is a small, flat, textured stitch. It is useful for backgrounds and borders because it halves so well it will conform to any space. It has a firm backing and will work on any canvas. The same amount of wool will be needed for this stitch as would be needed for the half cross stitch on the same canvas.

The stitch does bias the canvas if worked too tightly, therefore if it is to be used on a rug or wall hanging, a frame is recommended. Work all the small stitches first, basketweave style. Work the long strokes in horizontal or vertical rows to minimize the bias pull.

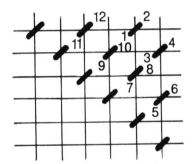 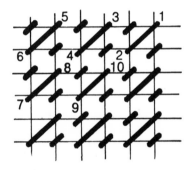

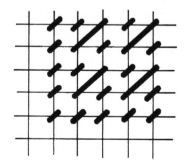

Mosaic Stitch

THE LONG-ARMED CROSS STITCH looks like a fat braid laid on the canvas. There is very little wool on the back of the canvas which is an advantage if the stitch is to be used as border. If bulky stitches are used near the edge of needlework it is hard to sew when finishing your project. The stitch is worked from left to right (the reverse for left-handers). If worked row on row there is a tendency for it to bias the canvas, in which case a frame is recommended. The same amount of wool is required in your needle as for the half cross stitch on the same canvas. Any canvas will do.

Start each row with a cross stitch, and finish with a little "fake" stitch. The stitch should be stroked on the surface of the canvas so that the needle goes in and out in one thrust from right to left.

Long-Armed Cross Stitch

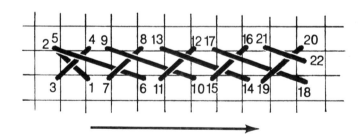

The long-armed cross stitch

Two-color herringbone stitch

THE TWO-COLOR HERRINGBONE STITCH is a very decorative stitch, good for borders or just by itself for the pattern it makes. It is worked in two journeys across the canvas, first with one color and then with the other. Because there is a line of unstitched mesh under each row of the stitch the canvas has a tendency to buckle in. Care must be taken that your stitches are worked loosely enough to combat this. A frame, of course, would help.

The stitch fits most comfortable on two-thread and leno canvases. It is difficult to work on canvas finer than ten mesh, and rug canvas is ideal. More wool will be needed in your needle than for the half cross stitch on the same canvas, especially when the stitch is worked as a row by itself. There is not much backing to this stitch or the following one. It is worked from left to right (the reverse for left-handers). The stitch should be stroked with one thrust of the needle from right to left, thus: 2-3, 4-5, 6-7 in the diagram.

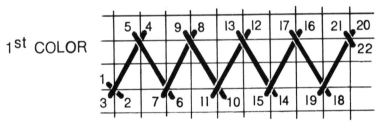

Two-Color Herringbone Stitch

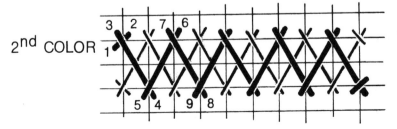

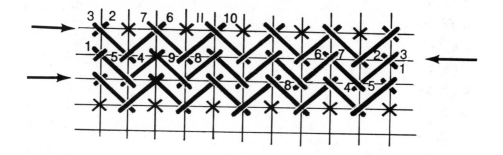

Reverse Herringbone

THE REVERSE HERRINGBONE looks like weaving viewed diagonally. The stitch does not bias the canvas, and provides only a light backing to it. A little more wool is needed in your needle than with the half cross stitch on the same canvas. Leno or a two-thread canvas accommodates the stitch the best. Because it is hard to find the empty top row of mesh under the previous row of stitching, do not work the stitch on fine mesh canvases. Ten mesh or less will be easiest.

To start, over every other mesh on the top row, work a small cross stitch. The top stroke of these stitches should be slanting toward the right. Work the first row of herringbone from left to right. The second row does not need the small cross stitch. Work it from right to left. Continue back and forth to the end of the allotted space. Then fill in the spaces with the small cross stitches again.

The reverse herringbone stitch

The point de tresse stitch

THE POINT DE TRESSE STITCH (modified) is a very effective border stitch because of its bulky look. Worked in stripes it is attractive too, but it is too heavy-looking for a backgrounding. It can be worked on any canvas and uses no more wool in the needle than the half cross stitch on the same kind of canvas. It provides a firm backing to the canvas, and does not bias.

Keep your wool untwisted so that it will lie flat and neat. The tension should be on the loose side to make the stitch sit up on the canvas, and also to prevent buckling. In step C, stitch 1-2 is laid in the same mesh as step A's 5-6.

Point de Tresse Stitch

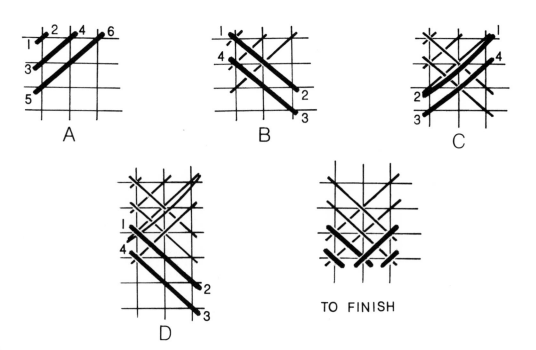

TURKEY WORK is essentially a shaggy rug stitch but it is also a marvelous stitch to use for lion manes, sheep fleeces, owl eyebrows, and Teddy Bear bodies. It can be worked on any canvas. On two-thread canvas a single stitch can be worked over one set of two threads to make a very dense pile or nap. Ordinarily the stitch is worked over two threads of mono canvas and leno canvas or two sets of threads of two-thread canvases. The space allotted for turkey work must be counted out to make sure that it is divisible by two because the stitch does not halve.

Turkey work

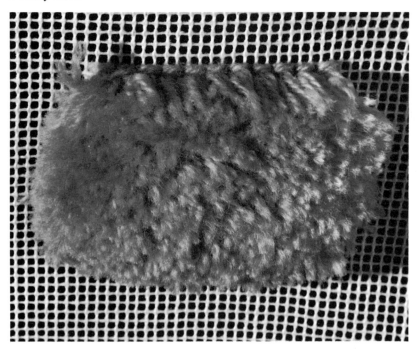

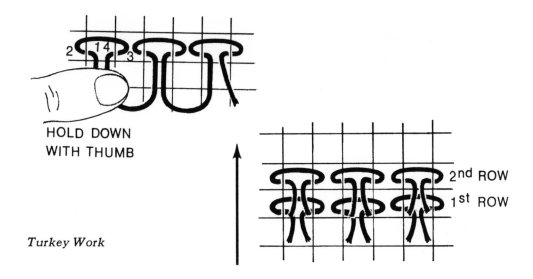

HOLD DOWN
WITH THUMB

Turkey Work

2nd ROW

1st ROW

Use the same amount of wool in your needle as you do for the half cross stitch on the same canvas. The stitch does not bias the canvas. Turkey work should be the very last stitch worked on your canvas, otherwise you must fight to keep the nap from tangling in nearby stitches. The stitch should be worked from the bottom of the canvas up again so that the nap won't get in your way. Basically what you are doing is knotting loops on canvas with a needle. The stitch is made with two strokes of the needle. The second stroke is pulled tightly to secure the knot. Your thumb will serve as the gauge for the loops, holding down the previous stitch as you work the next. Do not cut the loops until all the turkey work is done. Trim it with shears, but not too close. To give it a fuzzy look, hold the canvas near a steaming tea-kettle spout.

79

A collection of small things to make in needlepoint features a vegetable theme. Starting from upper left going clockwise: hanging kitchen scissors, key chain fob, glasses case, magnifying glass cover, pencil case and a comb case. All of them are from Greengage Designs of Washington, D. C.

Chapter Four

Blocking

How much you have to block your canvas on completion depends on just how biased it is. If it is just slightly askew, a steam pressing will suffice. Lay your canvas face down on the ironing board, unless there is turkey work on it. Then lay it face up. Use a damp pressing cloth over the canvas, and go over it with a warm iron completely (except in the turkey work area). Tug from side to side until you can see that the alignment is straight. Then press once more with the pressing cloth. Let the canvas dry for a few hours before going on to the finishing process.

A canvas that is more biased will have to be dampened more and tacked down to dry. For this process you will need an old towel or pillow case, a drawing board or piece of wall board, push pins or aluminum carpet tacks. The necessity for aluminum tacks is to prevent rust on your canvas which occurs if you use common tacks. If aluminum tacks are not obtainable, use copper ones. Only a slight green stain will result.

Wet the towel or pillow case thoroughly and roll your canvas up in it. Set it aside for three or four hours and then check to see how much moisture the canvas has absorbed. Dampening it this way instead of immersing it completely loosens the sizing in

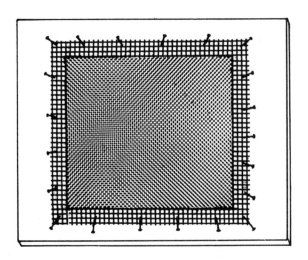

Blocking

the canvas instead of removing it. Hopefully it will prevent runnable paints from running.

When the canvas is thoroughly damp, tug it from side to side until it lines up the way you want it more or less. Cover the drawing board or wall board with brown paper or paper towels and start tacking the canvas to the board. Tack in each corner. The tacks should be placed between the canvas threads, not through them. This is to make sure the threads are not cut; for this reason staples will not do. The tacks should be placed about a half inch from the completed needlework. After cornering the canvas with tacks, put tacks in between, then every quarter, and so on around the canvas, tugging and pulling to make the canvas line up true.

You should end up with tacks about an inch apart, perhaps half an inch apart in some places. It does not really matter whether the canvas is face up or down for this operation. Except

82

of course, if there is turkey work on it, the canvas should be face up. Let the canvas dry about twenty-four hours before removing it from the board.

Total immersion is the final resort for a canvas that is really biased. Two blockings may be necessary to achieve any semblance of straightness, and then that may not last. If the canvas threads are "tied" into a biased position by the wool, there is nothing you can do except wish you had used a frame.

Do not soak the canvas. It is an invitation for the coloring medium or wool to run. Simply wet it completely in tepid or cold water. If the canvas is dirty, now is the time to wash it in Woolite. Wrap the canvas in a dry towel and squeeze the excess water out of it. Tug and pull as described before and then proceed with the tacking.

Finishing

Detailed directions for specific projects are beyond the scope of this book. However, the following are some general suggestions on various way of finishing needlepoint projects.

One of the simplest ways is that used for a rug or wall hanging—hemming the edges back. First machine stitch or liquid latex (Rug-Sta or Spee-Dee) the canvas an inch and a half away from the needlework. This is to prevent its ravelling as you work on it. Trim away the excess canvas close to the treated or machine-stitched edge. This is a good thing to do before mounting almost any needlepoint project.

To hem, fold the canvas back on the last row of stitching. Select a row of mesh to follow and whip stitch the bare canvas to the backs of completed stitches, being careful not to come

83

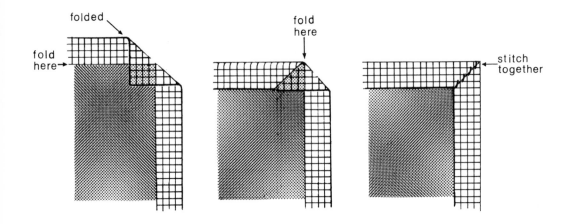

Mitred Corner

through on the surface. Use cotton thread or cotton carpet thread. Tuck a strip of Stitch Witchery between the back of the completed work and the aforementioned canvas hem, baste it in place and hem.

Before you get to the corner, trim it to within five mesh of the needlework, diagonally. Fold the remaining corner canvas down diagonally. The hem you have been working on and the one you will be working on around the corner will create when folded two matching diagonal edges. Whip stitch them together. This makes a mitred corner. Iron the folded edges flat using a damp pressing cloth. If a lining is to be used, pre-shrink the material. It should be an even-weave fabric, like linen or Indian Head. Lay the needlepoint face down on a flat surface, the lining on top. Pin tack the entire surface of the lining and needle-

84

point to be certain that both are flat and even. Fold the edge of the lining under and blind stitch around the edges, stitching into the bare canvas and the outside-edge needlepoint stitches. Only when the blind stitching is completed should you remove the pins.

Another simple method of finishing a needlepoint project is with the binding stitch. This stitch may be used over a single edge such as the mouth of an eyeglass case or the edges of a rug. It can also be used to join two pieces of canvas if the edges of each piece you wish to join have the exact same number of mesh. The stitch makes a neat edging around coasters and doll house rugs and a good join for totes, purses, and pin-cushions.

Fold your canvas on the last line of mesh right next to the needlepoint. Fold along one set of mesh for two-thread canvas, penelope, and leno canvas. Fold along two threads of mesh for mono canvas. The stitch is worked from left to right with the wrong side of the work facing you. The resulting stitch is a neat braid which will then slant toward the correct side of the work. You will find that you need less wool in your needle than you do for the half cross stitch on the same canvas.

The binding stitch

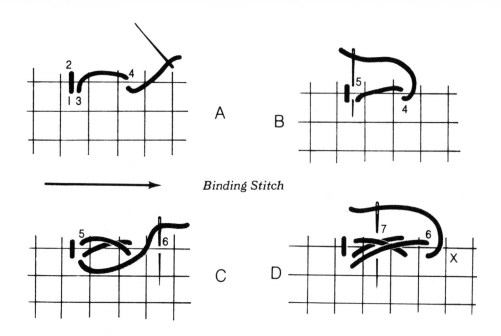

Binding Stitch

BINDING STITCH. The needle is always pointing toward you with the binding stitch. Fasten your wool in the backs of nearby completed stitches. Make a beginning stitch over the folded edge to start (diagram A, 1-2). Skip the next empty mesh and insert the needle into the next mesh (diagram A, 3-4). Go back into the mesh where you made your beginning stitches (diagram B, 4-5). The next stitch is forward again into the next empty mesh (diagram C, 5-6). Go back into the empty mesh next door to your starting mesh (diagram D, 6-7). The next stitch will go forward to X. Follow the steps in diagrams C and D on up the edge of the canvas. The rule to remember with this stitch is that when you go forward it is always into the next empty mesh. When you are heading back, skip one mesh before inserting the needle.

86

When you use up all the wool in your needle try to stop on a forward stitch. Bring the needle through to the wrong side of the canvas and run the wool out into the backs of nearby completed stitches. Start the new thread as close as you can to the old by running it up through completed stitches. Bring it out by that forward stitch just as if it were the continuation of the old thread. Go on stitching as before. When you are finished you may trim the excess canvas to within four or five mesh of the binding stitch.

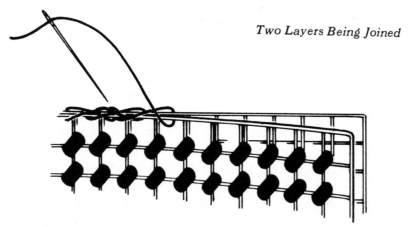

Two Layers Being Joined

To join two pieces of canvas, the mesh count must be exactly the same on both pieces. Again, you should fold the canvas back on the appropriate mesh nearest the needlepoint on both pieces. Then hold the pieces wrong side together and, matching mesh for mesh, work the binding stitch just as if you were working over a single edge. This join produces a "sharp" edge and thus is not suitable for a flat seam join.

87

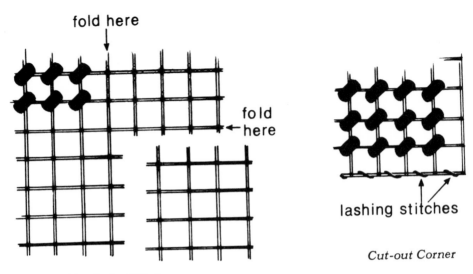

fold here

fold
← here

lashing stitches

Cut-out Corner

Corner Ready for Stitches

You may prepare your canvas for the binding stitch before you work your needlework if you wish. Just fold the canvas back five or six mesh from the planned needlepoint stitches. Baste it flat with cotton thread. Match mesh for mesh so that it looks as if there were just one layer of canvas there. Then work your needlework right up to the folded mesh or set of mesh over which the binding stitch will later be worked.

To turn a corner with the binding stitch the corner must first be prepared. Trim the excess canvas to within four or five mesh of the fold. Gently cut out the corner of the canvas, leaving one set of mesh next to the completed work. Fold the canvas, one piece overlapping the other, and then using cotton thread stitch the cut edge to the folded edge. There should now be a row of mesh set up for the binding stitch all the way around the corner. Work around the corner just as you would on the straightaway.

A sewing machine is helpful for other ways of finishing. To

sew material to needlepoint it is best to stitch right into the last outside row of completed stitches. This way bare canvas will not show through when the seam is opened. This is the method you would use to make flat knife-edge pillows with material backs or pin-cushions. Lay the backing material face down over the needlepoint, face up. Pin the edges. Machine stitch the two together with the needlepoint on the top so that you can see to stitch in the outside row of stitches. Leave a five-inch gap in your machine stitching so that you can turn your project right side out and stuff it. Trim the excess canvas away to within three quarters of an inch of the work. Quilt backing or old panty hose with the elastic cut off make an inexpensive stuffing. After stuffing, blind stitch the gap.

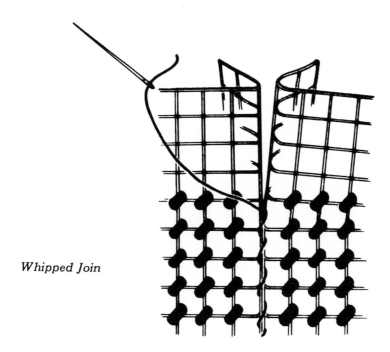

Whipped Join

Two layers of needlepoint may be sewn together by machine, again sewing through the outside row of stitches. This method would be used for the side seam of an eyeglass case, for instance. Another way of handling the seam is to fold back the canvas along one row of mesh on each side. Matching mesh for mesh, whip stitch the two rows of folded canvas together with cotton thread. Then, using matching background wool, work a row of quickpoint stitches up the single row of mesh created by whipping the two together. Press the seam flat, using a damp pressing cloth.

Cording

Cording makes a very nice trim for the edges of pillows and eyeglass cases. Following are directions for making a knotted and a knitted cording. For your first try on the knotted cording two colors are recommended. This way it is easier to tell which thread to handle. It takes about a foot of each of the two colors of wool to produce three inches of finished cording in Persian wool. The wool, incidentally, must be in two long continuous pieces.

Knot a small loop in one color of the wool, pull a loop of the other color through the first color and pull tightly on the strand of the first color. Pull a loop of the first color through the loop of the other color and pull tightly on the other color's strand, and so forth. You loop with one color, pull on the strand of the other. To finish, thread the strand of either color through the loop and pull tightly. To sew on to your pillow or case, blind stitch with cotton thread, picking up consistently the same color and line of cording to stitch to the seam.

90

The knitted cording is similar to the spool knitting you did as a child, the only difference being that it is worked over just two prongs. If you do not have a corder or lucet, make one out of two finishing nails driven into a small rectangle of wood about one and a half inches wide, an inch thick, and two or three inches long. Drive the nails down until about three-quarters of an inch protrudes. Set them three-quarters of an inch apart and about a third of an inch from the edge.

It takes about seven inches of wool to make an inch of cording using Persian wool. The wool must be one long continuous piece; cut strands will not work. To start, knot a small loop in the wool and hook it over one horn or nail of the corder. Wrap the working strand around the other horn and back around the first horn. Wrap in a figure-eight motion or straight around, whichever you prefer. Lift the bottom thread over the top thread and off the horn, pull tightly on the working strand. Wrap the working strand around the other horn, lift the bottom thread over the top thread and off the horn, pull the working strand tightly. As you work from horn to horn, turn the corder in your hand. To finish, pull the working thread through the remaining loop on each horn.

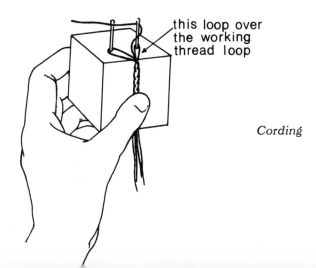

this loop over the working thread loop

Cording

The way to achieve a good tight cording is to pull the working strand firmly after every stitch. The first few stitches may be loose, but they will tighten up as the cording grows. To apply to your needlepoint project, select a line of stitches and follow that along as you blind stitch the cording to your project.

If you want to make tassels you will need a piece of cardboard on which to wind your wool. It should be as long as you want the tassel to be. Wind the wool around and around the card until you have as fat a tassel as you want. Thread a needle with two or three strands of wool and run it along the top of the card, catching up all the windings. Do this twice and then pull tightly, drawing together the windings. Make a knot to hold them secure. Do not cut the needled thread free yet; you will need it to attach the tassel to the corner of your project.

Wrap a strand of wool about an inch or so from the top of the tassel (or an appropriate distance from the top of the tassel depending on the length of the tassel). Wrap it around the tassel four or five times and pull it tightly, then knot it. Let the strands from the knot hang down with the rest of the tassel wool. Trim the bottom of the tassel evenly.

Repairs

If you make any mistakes in your stitching, do not despair; they can be corrected. If it is just a stitch or two, snip

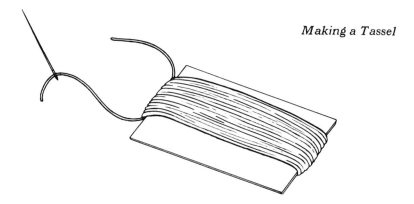

Making a Tassel

them out with slender-bladed embroidery scissors, being very careful not to cut the canvas. Using your needle as a pick, unwork five or six stitches on either side of your mistake. The reason for doing this is to produce enough wool to rethread the needle so that the cut ends can be fastened in on the back of the canvas. Restitch the now empty mesh with a fresh needleful of wool.

If the area is larger, you must still cut the stitches out, stitch by stitch, occasionally snipping from the back of the canvas to help free them. If the worst happens and you do cut a thread, this also can be repaired. Ravel a canvas thread from the edge of the canvas. Lash it down with cotton thread in line with the cut thread. Make sure your lashing stitches don't show through the front of the canvas. Dip a toothpick into a liquid latex like Rug-Sta and delicately cover the stubs of the cut thread. What you want to do is to glue the stubs together and at the same time fasten the ravelled thread to the stubs for re-enforcement. Allow the latex to dry for several hours before working over the mended area. Trim the re-enforcing thread to within a half inch or so of the mend. When you rework your stitches over this area, do so with a light hand.

A larger cut will have to be patched. Cut a piece of the same mesh canvas longer and wider than the cut by an inch or so. Tack the patch to the backs of completed stitches nearby or to the bare canvas so that the mesh match layer on layer exactly. Treat the cut stubs with latex on a toothpick to prevent any raveling; try to touch each intersection of the mesh. Allow the latex to dry for several hours. Work through both layers of canvas for three or four stitches on either side of the cut, and lightly and carefully over the cut. Some of the excess canvas of the patch may be trimmed away.

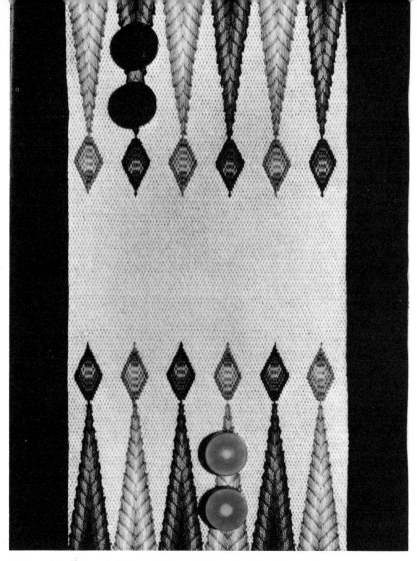

Aileen Sterling of Chevy Chase, Maryland, designed and worked the backgammon board in bargello and brick stitch. The points are in shades of green and gold, the background is eggshell.

Bibliography

BIRRELL, VERLA, *The Textile Arts*, New York: Harper & Row, 1959

BIRREN, FABER, *Creative Color*, New York: Van Nostrand Reinhold, 1961

GARTNER, LOUIS J., JR., *Needlepoint Design*, New York: William Morrow & Company, 1970

GIBBON, M. A., *Canvas Work*, London: G. Bell and Sons Ltd., 1965

SCOTT, ROBERT GILLAM, *Design Fundamentals*, New York: McGraw-Hill Book Company, 1951

THOMAS, MARY, *Mary Thomas's Embroidery Book*, New York: Gramercy Publishing Company, 1936

Handbook of Designs and Motifs, introduction by P. K. Thomajan, New York: Tudor Publishing Company, 1950

Recommended Reading

HANLEY, HOPE, *New Methods in Needlepoint*, New York: Charles Scribner's Sons, 1966

PERRONE, LISBETH, *The New World of Needlepoint*, New York: Random House, 1972

SNOOK, BARBARA, *Florentine Embroidery*, New York: Charles Scribner's Sons, 1967

Manufacturers and Wholesalers

Embroidery Paints:
Deco-Write
The Craftint Mfg. Company
Cleveland, Ohio 44112

Wool and canvas:
The DMC Corporation
107 Trumbull Street
Elizabeth, New Jersey 07206

Nantucket Needleworks
Nantucket Island, Massachusetts 02554

Paternayan Bros., Inc.
312 East 95th Street
New York, N. Y. 10028

Scandinavian Art Handicraft
7696 Camargo Road, Madeira
Cincinnati, Ohio 45243

Joan Toggitt, Inc.
1170 Broadway, Room 406
New York, N. Y. 10001

Shop-by-mail craft books:
The Unicorn
Box 645
Rockville, Maryland 20851